PRACTICE REC
AND ASSIGNMENT BOOK

This Assignment Book belongs to:

Name _____

Address _____

City/State/Zip _____

Phone Number _____

Teacher _____ Phone_____

LIST OF COMPOSERS

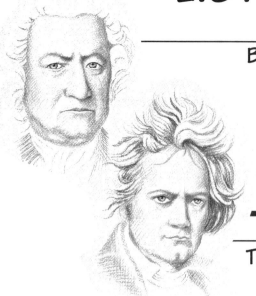

Baroque Period (1600–1750)

Johann Sebastian Bach (1685–1750) Germany
François Couperin (1668–1733) France
George Frideric Handel (1685–1759) Germany
Henry Purcell (1658–1695) England
Jean-Philippe Rameau (1683–1764) France
Domenico Scarlatti (1685–1757) Italy
Georg Philipp Telemann (1681–1767) Germany

Transitional Pre–Classic

Carl Phillip Emmanuel Bach (1710–1784) Germany
Johann Christian Bach (1735–1782) Germany
Johann Hässler (1747–1822) Germany
Johann Kirnberger (1721–1783) Germany
Leopold Mozart (1719–1787) Austria
Wilhelm Friedemann Bach (1710–1784) Germany

Classical Period (1750–1825)

Ludwig van Beethoven (1779–1827) Germany
Muzio Clementi (1752–1832) Italy
Antonio Diabelli (1781–1858) Italy
Franz Joseph Haydn (1732–1809) Austria
Friedrich Kuhlau (1786–1832) Germany
Wolfgang Amadeus Mozart (1757–1791) Austria
Daniel Türk (1756–1813) Germany

Romantic Period (1800–1900)

Johannes Brahms (1833–1897) Germany
Friedrich Burgmüller (1806–1874) Austria
Frédéric Chopin (1810–1849) Poland
Edvard Grieg (1843–1907) Norway
Cornelius Gurlitt (1820–1901) Germany
Stephen Heller (1813–1888) Hungary
Theodor Kullak (1818–1882) Germany
Franz Liszt (1811–1886) Hungary
Felix Mendelssohn (1809–1847) Germany
Modest Mussorgsky (1839–1881) Russia
Camille Saint-Saëns (1835–1921) France
Franz Schubert (1797–1828) Austria
Robert Schumann (1810–1856) Germany
Peter Ilyich Tchaikovsky (1840–1893) Russia

Transitional Late Romantic and Impressionistic

Claude Debussy (1862–1918) France
Gabriel Fauré (1845–1942) France
Enrique Granados (1867–1916) Spain
Scott Joplin (1869–1917) U.S.A.
Edward MacDowell (1861–1908) U.S.A.
Sergei Rachmaninoff (1873–1943) Russia
Maurice Ravel (1875–1937) France
Erik Satie (1866–1925) France
Alexander Scriabin (1872–1915) Russia
Joaquin Turina (1882–1949) Spain

Contemporary Period (1900–present)

Samuel Barber (1910–1981) U.S.A.
Béla Bartók (1881–1945) Hungary
Dave Brubeck (1920–) U.S.A.
Aaron Copland (1900–1990) U.S.A.
Norman Dello-Joio (1913–) U.S.A.
George Gershwin (1898–1937) U.S.A.
Alberto Ginastera (1916–1983) Argentina
Alexander Gretchaninoff (1864–1956) Russia
Paul Hindemith (1895–1963) Germany
Charles Ives (1870–1962) U.S.A.
Dimitri Kabalevsky (1904–1987) Russia
Aram Khachaturian (1903–1978) Russia
Samuel Maykapar (1867–1938) Russia
Darius Milhaud (1892–1974) France
Gian-Carlo Menotti (1911–) Italy/U.S.A.
Vincent Persichetti (1915–1987) U.S.A.
Francis Poulenc (1899–1963) France
Sergei Prokofiev (1891–1953) Russia
Arnold Schoenberg (1874–1951) Austria
Dimitri Shostakovich (1906–1975) Russia
Robert Starer (1924–2001) U.S.A.
Igor Stravinsky (1882–1971) Russia/U.S.A.
Alexandre Tansman (1897–1986) France
Alexander Tcherepnin (1899–1977) Russia/U.S.A.
Heitor Villa Lobos (1887–1964) Brazil

PERFORMANCE-READY
PIECES
Repertoire List

Composition	Composer	Date

MEMORIZED PIECES

Composition	Composer	Date

PERFORMANCE RECORD

Event	Composition	Composer	Date

LESSON ASSIGNMENT

Date _____

Practice Record ✓	SUN	MON	TUE	WED	THUR	FRI	SAT	Parent Signature and Notes to the Teacher

LESSON ASSIGNMENT

Date _____

Practice Record ✓	SUN	MON	TUE	WED	THUR	FRI	SAT	Parent Signature and Notes to the Teacher

LESSON ASSIGNMENT

Date _____

Practice Record ✓	SUN	MON	TUE	WED	THUR	FRI	SAT	Parent Signature and Notes to the Teacher

LESSON ASSIGNMENT

Date _____

Practice Record ✓	SUN	MON	TUE	WED	THUR	FRI	SAT	Parent Signature and Notes to the Teacher

LESSON ASSIGNMENT

Date _____

Practice Record ✓	SUN	MON	TUE	WED	THUR	FRI	SAT	Parent Signature and Notes to the Teacher

LESSON ASSIGNMENT

Date _____

Practice Record ✓	SUN	MON	TUE	WED	THUR	FRI	SAT	Parent Signature and Notes to the Teacher

LESSON ASSIGNMENT

Date _____

Practice Record ✔	SUN	MON	TUE	WED	THUR	FRI	SAT	Parent Signature and Notes to the Teacher

LESSON ASSIGNMENT

Date _____

Practice Record ✔	SUN	MON	TUE	WED	THUR	FRI	SAT	Parent Signature and Notes to the Teacher

LESSON ASSIGNMENT

Date _____

Practice Record ✔	SUN	MON	TUE	WED	THUR	FRI	SAT	Parent Signature and Notes to the Teacher

LESSON ASSIGNMENT

Date _____

Practice Record ✔	SUN	MON	TUE	WED	THUR	FRI	SAT	Parent Signature and Notes to the Teacher

LESSON ASSIGNMENT

Date _____

Practice Record ✔	SUN	MON	TUE	WED	THUR	FRI	SAT	Parent Signature and Notes to the Teacher

LESSON ASSIGNMENT

Date _____

Practice Record ✔	SUN	MON	TUE	WED	THUR	FRI	SAT	Parent Signature and Notes to the Teacher

LESSON ASSIGNMENT

Date _____

Practice Record ✓	SUN	MON	TUE	WED	THUR	FRI	SAT	Parent Signature and Notes to the Teacher

LESSON ASSIGNMENT

Date _____

Practice Record ✓	SUN	MON	TUE	WED	THUR	FRI	SAT	Parent Signature and Notes to the Teacher

LESSON ASSIGNMENT

Date _____

Practice Record ✓	SUN	MON	TUE	WED	THUR	FRI	SAT	Parent Signature and Notes to the Teacher

LESSON ASSIGNMENT

Date _____

Practice Record ✓	SUN	MON	TUE	WED	THUR	FRI	SAT	Parent Signature and Notes to the Teacher

LESSON ASSIGNMENT

Date _____

Practice Record ✔	SUN	MON	TUE	WED	THUR	FRI	SAT	Parent Signature and Notes to the Teacher

LESSON ASSIGNMENT

Date _____

Practice Record ✔	SUN	MON	TUE	WED	THUR	FRI	SAT	Parent Signature and Notes to the Teacher

LESSON ASSIGNMENT

Date _____

Practice Record ✓	SUN	MON	TUE	WED	THUR	FRI	SAT	Parent Signature and Notes to the Teacher

LESSON ASSIGNMENT

Date _____

Practice Record ✓	SUN	MON	TUE	WED	THUR	FRI	SAT	Parent Signature and Notes to the Teacher

LESSON ASSIGNMENT

Date _____

Practice Record ✓	SUN	MON	TUE	WED	THUR	FRI	SAT	Parent Signature and Notes to the Teacher

LESSON ASSIGNMENT

Date _____

Practice Record ✓	SUN	MON	TUE	WED	THUR	FRI	SAT	Parent Signature and Notes to the Teacher

LESSON ASSIGNMENT

Date _____

Practice Record ✓	SUN	MON	TUE	WED	THUR	FRI	SAT	Parent Signature and Notes to the Teacher

LESSON ASSIGNMENT

Date _____

Practice Record ✓	SUN	MON	TUE	WED	THUR	FRI	SAT	Parent Signature and Notes to the Teacher

LESSON ASSIGNMENT

Date _____

Practice Record ✓	SUN	MON	TUE	WED	THUR	FRI	SAT	Parent Signature and Notes to the Teacher

LESSON ASSIGNMENT

Date _____

Practice Record ✓	SUN	MON	TUE	WED	THUR	FRI	SAT	Parent Signature and Notes to the Teacher

LESSON ASSIGNMENT

Date _____

Practice Record ✔	SUN	MON	TUE	WED	THUR	FRI	SAT	Parent Signature and Notes to the Teacher

LESSON ASSIGNMENT

Date _____

Practice Record ✔	SUN	MON	TUE	WED	THUR	FRI	SAT	Parent Signature and Notes to the Teacher

LESSON ASSIGNMENT

Date _____

Practice Record ✓	SUN	MON	TUE	WED	THUR	FRI	SAT	Parent Signature and Notes to the Teacher

LESSON ASSIGNMENT

Date _____

Practice Record ✓	SUN	MON	TUE	WED	THUR	FRI	SAT	Parent Signature and Notes to the Teacher

LESSON ASSIGNMENT

Date _____

Practice Record ✓	SUN	MON	TUE	WED	THUR	FRI	SAT	Parent Signature and Notes to the Teacher

LESSON ASSIGNMENT

Date _____

Practice Record ✓	SUN	MON	TUE	WED	THUR	FRI	SAT	Parent Signature and Notes to the Teacher

LESSON ASSIGNMENT

Date _____

Practice Record ✓	SUN	MON	TUE	WED	THUR	FRI	SAT	Parent Signature and Notes to the Teacher

LESSON ASSIGNMENT

Date _____

Practice Record ✓	SUN	MON	TUE	WED	THUR	FRI	SAT	Parent Signature and Notes to the Teacher

LESSON ASSIGNMENT

Date _____

Practice Record ✔	SUN	MON	TUE	WED	THUR	FRI	SAT	Parent Signature and Notes to the Teacher

LESSON ASSIGNMENT

Date _____

Practice Record ✔	SUN	MON	TUE	WED	THUR	FRI	SAT	Parent Signature and Notes to the Teacher

LESSON ASSIGNMENT

Date _____

Practice Record ✔	SUN	MON	TUE	WED	THUR	FRI	SAT	Parent Signature and Notes to the Teacher

LESSON ASSIGNMENT

Date _____

Practice Record ✔	SUN	MON	TUE	WED	THUR	FRI	SAT	Parent Signature and Notes to the Teacher

LESSON ASSIGNMENT

Date _____

Practice Record ✓	SUN	MON	TUE	WED	THUR	FRI	SAT	Parent Signature and Notes to the Teacher

LESSON ASSIGNMENT

Date _____

Practice Record ✓	SUN	MON	TUE	WED	THUR	FRI	SAT	Parent Signature and Notes to the Teacher

LESSON ASSIGNMENT

Date _____

Practice Record ✓	SUN	MON	TUE	WED	THUR	FRI	SAT	Parent Signature and Notes to the Teacher

LESSON ASSIGNMENT

Date _____

Practice Record ✓	SUN	MON	TUE	WED	THUR	FRI	SAT	Parent Signature and Notes to the Teacher

LESSON ASSIGNMENT

Date _____

Practice Record ✓	SUN	MON	TUE	WED	THUR	FRI	SAT	Parent Signature and Notes to the Teacher

LESSON ASSIGNMENT

Date _____

Practice Record ✓	SUN	MON	TUE	WED	THUR	FRI	SAT	Parent Signature and Notes to the Teacher

LESSON ASSIGNMENT

Date _____

Practice Record ✔	SUN	MON	TUE	WED	THUR	FRI	SAT	Parent Signature and Notes to the Teacher

LESSON ASSIGNMENT

Date _____

Practice Record ✔	SUN	MON	TUE	WED	THUR	FRI	SAT	Parent Signature and Notes to the Teacher

LESSON ASSIGNMENT

Date _____

Practice Record ✔	SUN	MON	TUE	WED	THUR	FRI	SAT	Parent Signature and Notes to the Teacher

LESSON ASSIGNMENT

Date _____

Practice Record ✔	SUN	MON	TUE	WED	THUR	FRI	SAT	Parent Signature and Notes to the Teacher

LESSON ASSIGNMENT

Date _____

Practice Record ✓	SUN	MON	TUE	WED	THUR	FRI	SAT	Parent Signature and Notes to the Teacher

LESSON ASSIGNMENT

Date _____

Practice Record ✓	SUN	MON	TUE	WED	THUR	FRI	SAT	Parent Signature and Notes to the Teacher

LESSON ASSIGNMENT   Date _____

Practice Record ✓	SUN	MON	TUE	WED	THUR	FRI	SAT	Parent Signature and Notes to the Teacher

LESSON ASSIGNMENT   Date _____

Practice Record ✓	SUN	MON	TUE	WED	THUR	FRI	SAT	Parent Signature and Notes to the Teacher

SCALE FINGERING REFERENCE CHART

MAJOR SCALES

C, G, D, A, E
RH   123 1234 123 12345
LH   54321 321 4321 321

B, C♭
RH   123 1234 123 12345
LH   4321 4321 321 4321

F♯, G♭
RH   234 123 1234 123 12
LH   4321 321 4321 321 4

C♯, D♭
RH   23 1234 123 1234 12
LH   321 4321 321 4321 3

F
RH   1234 123 1234 1234
LH   54321 321 4321 321

B♭
RH   4 123 1234 123 1234
LH   321 4321 321 4321 3

E♭
RH   3 1234 123 1234 123
LH   321 4321 321 4321 3

A♭
RH   34 123 1234 123 123
LH   321 4321 321 4321 3

MINOR SCALES (Harmonic form)

a, e, d, c, g
RH   123 1234 123 12345
LH   54321 321 4321 321

b
RH   123 1234 123 12345
LH   4321 4321 321 4321

f♯
RH   34 123 1234 123 123
LH   4321 321 4321 321 4

c♯
RH   34 123 1234 123 123
LH   321 4321 321 4321 3

g♯, a♭
RH   34 123 1234 123 123
LH   321 4321 321 4321 3

f
RH   1234 123 1234 1234
LH   54321 321 4321 321

d♯, e♭
RH   3 1234 123 1234 123
LH   21 4321 321 4321 32

b♭, a♯
RH   4 123 1234 123 1234
LH   21 321 4321 321 432

MAJOR AND MINOR SCALES

SCALES, CHORDS, AND FIVE-FINGER PATTERNS

✓ Place a check mark on the line when you have learned and memorized the scales, five-finger patterns, and chords.

	Scale	Five-Finger Pattern	Chords		Scale	Five-Finger Pattern	Chords
C Major	____	____	____	F Major	____	____	____
A minor	____	____	____	D minor	____	____	____
G Major	____	____	____	B♭ Major	____	____	____
E minor	____	____	____	G minor	____	____	____
D Major	____	____	____	E♭ Major	____	____	____
B minor	____	____	____	C minor	____	____	____
A Major	____	____	____	A♭ Major	____	____	____
F♯ minor	____	____	____	F minor	____	____	____
E Major	____	____	____	D♭ Major	____	____	____
C♯ minor	____	____	____	B♭ minor	____	____	____
B Major	____	____	____	G♭ Major	____	____	____
G♯ minor	____	____	____	E♭ minor	____	____	____
F♯ Major	____	____	____	C♭ Major	____	____	____
D♯ minor	____	____	____	A♭ minor	____	____	____

MAJOR TRIAD
CHORD CHART

Root Position and Chord Inversions

Practice each of the major chords, first as broken chords as shown above, then as block chords. For example:

LOONEY TUNES PIANO LIBRARY
All the hottest hits you want to play!
Makes practicing more FUN than ever!
Vibrant duet parts for all Primer Level books.
Arrangements by Tom Roed, Jerry Ray, Eugenie Rocherolle, Gail Lew, Dan Coates, and more top composers and arrangers correlated with all piano methods.

PRIMER LEVEL (Early Elementary)
BUGS BUNNY'S AWESOME SONGS
This Is It! (from "THE BUGS BUNNY SHOW")
Lean on Me
Theme from Jurassic Park
Secret Agent Man
Animaniacs
I Got Rhythm
Rock Around the Clock
I Want It That Way (BACKSTREET BOYS)
Somewhere Out There (from "AN AMERICAN TAIL")
I Believe I Can Fly (from "SPACE JAM")
(ELM00110) and (ELM00110CD) with CD and MIDI disk

DAFFY DUCK'S SPECTACULAR SONGS
Theme from Inspector Gadget
Star Wars Main Title
Pinky & the Brain
Batman Theme
Strike Up the Band
The Teddy Bears' Picnic
Top Cat
Huckleberry Hound
Hello Muddah, Hello Faddah
Traveling Animaniacs
(EL9902) and (EL9902CD) with CD and MIDI disk

SYLVESTER'S SNAPPY SONGS
The Lion Sleeps Tonight
Happy Birthday
Over the Rainbow
Take Me Out to the Ballgame
I Taut I Taw a Puddy-Tat
Singin' in the Bathtub
The Star-Spangled Banner
This Land Is Your Land
The Band Played On
I'd Like to Teach the World to Sing
The Yankee Doodle Boy
You're a Grand Old Flag
(EL9903) and (EL9903CD) with CD and MIDI disk

LEVEL ONE (Elementary)
ELMER FUDD'S FANTASTIC SONGS
The Lion Sleeps Tonight
Jeopardy Theme
Merrily We Roll Along (from "LOONEY TUNES")
Animal Crackers in My Soup
On the Good Ship Lollipop
The Chipmunk Song
Welcome Christmas (from "HOW THE GRINCH STOLE CHRISTMAS")
Once Upon a December (from "ANASTASIA")
The Rose
Don't Cry for Me Argentina (from "EVITA")
(ELM00111) and (ELM00111CD) with CD and MIDI disk

LEVEL ONE (Elementary) continued
PEPE LE PEW'S POPULAR SONGS
Peter Cottontail
High Hopes
Shape of My Heart (BACKSTREET BOYS)
Wind Beneath My Wings (BETTE MIDLER)
Tomorrow (from "ANNIE")
We're Off to See the Wizard (from "THE WIZARD OF OZ")
If I Only Had a Brain (from "THE WIZARD OF OZ")
Eye of the Tiger (from "ROCKY III")
We Are the World (MICHAEL JACKSON)
What a Wonderful World
(ELM01039) and (ELM01039CD) with CD and MIDI disk

TWEETY'S EASY LISTENING SONGS
I Believe I Can Fly (from "SPACE JAM")
La Bamba
Rock Around the Clock
Over the Rainbow
Puff the Magic Dragon
This Is It!
Stand by Me
Happy Birthday to You
Chopsticks
Singin' in the Rain
(EL9905) and (EL9905CD) with CD and MIDI disk

LEVEL TWO (Late Elementary)
TAZ'S TERRIFIC SONGS
Somewhere Out There
Don't Cry for Me Argentina (from "EVITA")
Talk to the Animals (from "DOCTOR DOOLITTLE")
Theme from Rocky
Woody Woodpecker
Lean on Me
Chitty Chitty Bang Bang
Merrily We Roll Along (from "THE BUGS BUNNY SHOW")
Theme from Inspector Gadget
(EL9904) and (EL9904CD) with CD and MIDI disk

SYLVESTER JR.'S JAZZY SONGS
Satin Doll
Girl from Ipanema
I Got Rhythm
When I Fall in Love
Misty
A Foggy Day
Don't Get Around Much Anymore
Mack the Knife
My Funny Valentine
Ain't Misbehavin'
(ELM01040) and (ELM01040CD) with CD and MIDI disk

LEVEL TWO (Late Elementary) continued
WILE E. COYOTE'S COLORFUL SONGS
I Will Survive
You Light Up My Life
Put On a Happy Face
If My Friends Could See Me Now!
The Pink Panther
Hooray for Hollywood
Linus and Lucy
Theme from "SUPERMAN"
Tomorrow (from "ANNIE")
At the Beginning (from "ANASTASIA")
(ELM00112) and (EL00112CD) with CD and MIDI disk

LEVEL THREE (Early Intermediate)
SCOOBY DOO'S UPBEAT SONGS
Scooby Doo Main Title
Cantina Band (from "STAR WARS")
Theme from New York, New York
Once Upon a December (from "ANASTASIA")
The Jetsons
Fame
Fascinating Rhythm
(EL9908) and (EL9908CD) with CD and MIDI disk

LOLA BUNNY'S BROADWAY SONGS
I Could Have Danced All Night (from "MY FAIR LADY")
On a Clear Day
I Want to Be Happy
I've Gotta Be Me
If I Were a Rich Man
Matchmaker (from "FIDDLER ON THE ROOF")
Singin' in the Rain
Strike Up the Band
Heart
Send in the Clowns (from "A LITTLE NIGHT MUSIC")
(ELM01041) and (ELM01041CD) with CD and MIDI disk

YOSEMITE SAM'S SENSATIONAL SONGS
James Bond Theme
Bailamos (ENRIQUE IGLESIAS)
Boogie Woogie Bugle Boy (BETTE MIDLER)
That's the Way It Is (CELINE DION)
Smooth (SANTANA featuring ROB THOMAS)
Show Me the Meaning of Being Lonely
        (BACKSTREET BOYS)
Looking Through Your Eyes (LeANN RIMES)
Ragtime (from "RAGTIME")
Believe (CHER)
(ELM00113) and (ELM00113CD) with CD and MIDI disk

LEVEL FOUR (Intermediate)
FOGHORN LEGHORN'S HOT HIT SONGS
Shape of My Heart (BACKSTREET BOYS)
The One (BACKSTREET BOYS)
Livin' La Vida Loca (RICKY MARTIN)
This I Promise You (★NSYNC)
Breathe (FAITH HILL)
I Turn to You (CHRISTINA AGUILERA)
Can't Take That Away (MARIAH CAREY)
Back at One (BRYAN McKNIGHT)
A Love Until the End of Time
    (PLACIDO DOMINGO & MAUREEN McGOVERN)
Oops!...I Did It Again (BRITNEY SPEARS)
(ELM01042) and (EL01042CD) with CD and MIDI disk

MARVIN THE MARTIAN'S MODERN SONGS
I Believe in You and Me (WHITNEY HOUSTON)
Angel Eyes (JIM BRICKMAN)
Because You Loved Me (CELINE DION)
I Still Believe (MARIAH CAREY)
The Prayer (ANDREA BOCELLI and CELINE DION)
Don't Cry for Me Argentina (from "EVITA")
What a Wonderful World
Dreaming of You (SELENA)
I Want It That Way (BACKSTREET BOYS)
(EL9906) and (EL9906CD) with CD and MIDI disk

ROAD RUNNER'S ADVENTURE SONGS
Star Wars
Theme from Inspector Gadget
Animaniacs
Linus and Lucy
Tiny Toon Adventures Theme
The Batman Theme
(Meet) The Flintstones
This Is It!
Mighty Mouse Theme
Jeopardy Theme
Tomorrow
Superman
The Pink Panther
We're Off to See the Wizard
 (EL9907) and (EL9907CD) with CD and MIDI disk

PORKY PIG'S CHRISTMAS SONGS
Have Yourself a Merry Little Christmas
Sleigh Ride
Let It Snow! Let It Snow! Let It Snow!
Winter Wonderland
I'll Be Home for Christmas
Santa Claus Is Comin' to Town
Home for the Holidays
God Rest Ye Merry, Gentlemen
Christmas Mem'ries
Good King Wenceslas
We Three Kings of Orient Are
(EL9909) and (EL9909CD) with CD and MIDI disk

BE PART OF A REAL BAND!
Just play along with the incredible background accompaniments on CD and MIDI disk

WB POPULAR PIANO LIBRARY

- **POPULAR HITS YOUR STUDENTS WANT TO PLAY!**
- **Exciting arrangements by EUGÉNIE ROCHEROLLE, TOM ROED, GAIL LEW, and LARRY MINSKY**
- **Carefully graded levels**
- **Dynamic CD and MIDI accompaniments by CHRIS LOBDELL**

JAZZ HITS, Level 3

Book Only (ELM04001)
Book, CD, and MIDI Disk
(ELM04001CD)

- Ja Da
- Charade
- All the Things You Are
- Sophisticated Lady
- Willow Weep for Me
- Someone to Watch Over Me
- Over the Rainbow
- I Got Rhythm
- Summertime
- Cast Your Fate to the Wind

MOVIE HITS, Level 3

Book Only (ELM04002)
Book, CD, and MIDI Disk
(ELM04002CD)

- Secret Agent Man
- Theme from *Inspector Gadget*
- Fawkes the Phoenix (from *Harry Potter and the Chamber of Secrets*)
- Theme from *Rocky*
- Star Wars (Main Theme)
- I Believe I Can Fly
- Hedwig's Theme (from *Harry Potter and the Sorcerer's Stone*)
- Flashdance . . . What a Feeling
- Over the Rainbow
- The Pink Panther
- Theme from *Jurassic Park*
- Somewhere Out There

MOVIE HITS, Level 4

Book Only (ELM04003)
Book, CD, and MIDI Disk
(ELM04003CD)

- James Bond Theme
- In Dreams (from *The Lord of the Rings: The Fellowship of the Ring*)
- Theme from *Fame*
- Harry's Wondrous World
- Theme from *E.T.: The Extra Terrestrial*
- At the Beginning
- Once Upon a December
- Raindrops Keep Fallin' on My Head
- Cantina Band (from *Star Wars®*)
- There You'll Be (from *Pearl Harbor*)
- Scooby-Doo, Where Are You?
- Theme from *Superman*

MOVIE HITS, Level 5

Book Only (ELM04004)
Book, CD, and MIDI Disk
(ELM04004CD)

- And All That Jazz (from *Chicago*)
- Where Are You Christmas? (from *How the Grinch Stole Christmas*)
- Because You Loved Me
- I Believe in You and Me
- The Greatest Love of All
- You Light Up My Life
- Hedwig's Theme (from *Harry Potter and the Sorcerer's Stone*)
- The Prayer
- Fawkes the Phoenix (from *Harry Potter and the Chamber of Secrets*)
- Looking Through Your Eyes
- Over the Rainbow

Warner Bros. Publications presents
WB Christian Piano Library

♪ **INSPIRE** your students with exciting and creative arrangements of modern-day worship songs, Sunday school favorites, and great hymns of faith.

♪ **TRAIN** and encourage your students to share their musical talent in children's church, Sunday school, and the church service.

♪ **ENCOURAGE** beginning students to participate in the worship service with the professional-sounding gospel duet accompaniments.

♪ **TEACH** rhythmic precision using the powerful worship band MIDI accompaniment disks created by internationally acclaimed composer and orchestrator Chris Lobdell.

AD1153 7/04

PEDAGOGICAL ENOUGH FOR THE STUDIO.
PROFESSIONAL ENOUGH FOR THE SANCTUARY.

Gail Lew

Chris Lobdell

Beatrice Miller

Eugénie Rocherolle

Worship & Praise, Primer Level
Arranged by Gail Lew and Chris Lobdell
Early-Elementary Piano Solos with Teacher Duets
Book and MIDI Disk (ELM01002)
God Is So Good • Jesus Loves Me • I've Got the Joy, Joy, Joy • Praise Him, Praise Him • Jesus, Name Above All Names • I Worship You, Almighty God • I Sing Praises • I Love You Lord • and more.

Worship & Praise, Level One
Arranged by Gail Lew and Chris Lobdell
Elementary Piano Solos with Teacher Duets
Book and MIDI Disk (ELM01003)
Jesus in the Morning • Give Me Oil in My Lamp • This Is the Day • Stand Up, Stand Up for Jesus • He Is Lord • Seek Ye First • Glorify Thy Name • He Is Exalted • Shout to the Lord • Come Just as You Are • and more.

Worship & Praise, Level Two
Arranged by Gail Lew and Chris Lobdell
Late-Elementary Piano Solos with Teacher Duets
Book and MIDI Disk (ELM01004)
Open the Eyes of My Heart • Jesus Name Above All Names • I Could Sing of Your Love Forever • This Little Light of Mine • I Have Decided to Follow Jesus • Jesus Is All the World to Me • O How He Loves You and Me • Above All • and more.

Worship & Praise, Level Three
Arranged by Beatrice A. Miller
Early-Intermediate Piano Solos (ELM01005)
Amazing Grace • Blessed Assurance • Fairest Lord Jesus • Jesus Loves Me • Morning Has Broken • Oh, How I Love Jesus • Savior, Like a Shepherd, Lead Us • This Is My Father's World • What a Friend We Have in Jesus.

With Praise & Thanks, Level Four
Arranged by Eugénie R. Rocherolle
Intermediate Piano Solos (ELM01006)
Be Still, My Soul • Be Thou My Vision • In the Garden • Sent Forth by God's Blessing • What Wondrous Love Is This? • Now Thank We All Our God • For All the Saints • Nearer My God to Thee • and more.

Worship & Praise, Level Five
Arranged by Beatrice Miller
Late-Intermediate Piano Solos (ELM01007)
I Surrender All • The Church's One Foundation • It Is Well with My Soul • Amazing Grace • How Great Thou Art • Jesus Walked This Lonesome Valley • Precious Lord, Take My Hand • Jesus Loves Me.

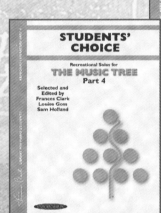 

THE PIANO MASTERS SERIES

Outstanding Editions of Essential Piano Repertoire

Warner Bros. Publications proudly presents a superb series of books
that contain original piano solos by master composers.

Each book features:
- The most frequently performed and favorite teaching pieces
- Careful editing for the correct performance, with fingerings and written-out ornaments
- A complete composer biography
- Beautiful cover art

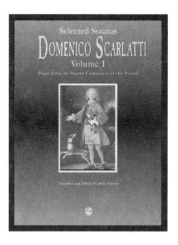

**Selections from the Notebook
for Anna Magdalena Bach
Johann Sebastian Bach**
(EL9916) Late Elementary

**Selected Works
Béla Bartók**
(ELM00028) Early Intermediate to
Intermediate

**Selected Works
Ludwig van Beethoven**
(ELM00027) Early Intermediate to
Intermediate

**Selections from
Burgmüller Studies
Opus 100 and 109**
(EL9923) Intermediate to Late Intermediate

**Selected Works
Frédéric Chopin**
(ELM00010) Early Intermediate to Intermediate

**Selected Sonatas
Muzio Clementi**
(ELM01012) Late Intermediate

**Selections from Lyric Pieces
Edvard Grieg**
(ELM00039) Late Intermediate

**Selected Works
Cornelius Gurlitt**
(ELM00012) Early Intermediate to
Intermediate

**Selected Sonatas
Franz Joseph Haydn**
(ELM01011) Early Advanced

**Selected Etudes
Stephen Heller**
(ELM00021) Intermediate

**Selected Sonatinas
Friedrich Kuhlau**
(ELM00040) Intermediate

**Selections from Pedal Preludes
Samuel Maykapar**
(ELM00048) Early Intermediate to
Intermediate

**Selected Songs Without Words
Felix Mendelssohn**
(ELM01010) Early Advanced

**Selected Works
Gian-Carlo Menotti
Poemetti**
(ELM03005) Intermediate to Late Intermediate

**Selected Works
Wolfgang Amadeus Mozart**
(ELM00026) Late Intermediate

**Selections from
Music for Children, Opus 65
Sergei Prokofiev**
(ELM00041) Intermediate

**Selected Sonatas
Domenico Scarlatti**
(ELM01008) Volume I
Late Intermediate
(ELM01009) Volume II
Late Intermediate

**Selections from
Album for the Young
Robert Schumann**
(EL9918) Intermediate

**Selections from
Album for the Young
Peter Ilyich Tchaikovsky**
(ELM00009) Early Intermediate to Intermediate

**Selected Sonatinas
Various Composers**
(ELM00037A) Volume I
Early Intermediate
(ELM00038) Volume II
Intermediate to Late Intermediate

MUSIC DICTIONARY

TERM	DEFINITION
accelerando	gradually faster, accelerate tempo
adagio	very slowly
andante	walking tempo
andantino	not quite as slow as *andante*
allegretto	not quite as lively as *allegro*
allegro	fast, quick, and lively
a tempo	return to the original tempo
cantabile	in a singing style
Coda	an added section that serves as an ending
con	with
con moto	with motion
crescendo (*cresc.*)	gradually louder
D.C. al Coda	return to the beginning, play to the *Coda* sign (⊕), then play the *Coda*
D.C. al Fine	return to the beginning and play to *Fine*
D.S. al Coda	return to the sign (𝄋) play to the *Coda* sign (⊕), then play the *Coda*
D.S. al Fine	return to the sign (𝄋) and play to *Fine*
decrescendo	gradually softer
diminuendo (*dim.*)	get softer
dolce	sweetly
enharmonic	pitches that sound the same but are named or spelled differently
espressivo	expressively
fine	the end
largo	stately, broadly, dignified, slowly
legato	smooth and connected
leggiero	lightly
marcato	marked
molto	much, very
motive	a short musical idea
moderato	moderate tempo
poco	little
presto	very fast tempo
ritard (*rit.*)	gradually slower
ritardando (*rit.*)	gradually slower
scherzando	jokingly, lightly, playfully
sforzando (*sfz*)	a sudden, sharp accent
simile	similarly, the same as
sostenuto	sustained, legato
subito	suddenly
tranquillo	peacefully, tranquil, calm
tre corde	release the soft pedal
una corda	depress the soft pedal (pedal on the left)
vivace	quick, lively, very fast